GW00862516

Kidscape

Howard Martin
Gaby Shenton
Cath Bracher-Giles

Illustrations by Roz Eirew

Sponsored by NATIONAL
LOTTERY
CHARITIES
BOARD

'WHAT YOU FEEL MATTERS,
WHAT YOU WANT MATTERS'

Introduction

We've been hoping you'd pick up this book. We've been thinking about it and writing it for some time. This book only exists thanks to the enormous courage of thousands of people who participated in our study into the longterm effects of bullying, funded by the National Lottery Charities Board. People wrote to us not just about the bullying they had suffered, but about ways they had found out of the pain.

Bullying hurts; that much we know. But do you also know that you can recover ? that the pain can recede ? that you can wake up in the morning and bounce like Tigger out of bed ? and that in time, the pain will actually go away ?

In this book, there are ideas of how you can start feeling better about yourself; how to think about the bullying and then, at a pace that suits you, move on. This book is crammed with ideas about things to do, think about and try from art to breathing, karate to visualisation. On every page, we have included a quote from someone who has come through bullying and spoken out about it. We welcome your suggestions too and will try to include them in future publications.

When I look back, I often think of things that I wish I had done but hadn't. I rarely look back on things I had tried and wish I hadn't. So, if there's any message, it's a challenge to try something new and positive and good for you.

You've done the hard bit; you've survived the bullying: you've got this far and you've got this book. Now, let the recovery and the fun begin.

Gaby Shenton
Project Leader & Assistant Director, Kidscape
National Lottery Charities Board sponsored project
'Longterm Effects of Bullying'

*'EXPERIENCE : IT'S NOT WHAT HAPPENS TO YOU,
IT'S WHAT YOU DO WITH WHAT HAPPENS TO YOU.'*

What is bullying?

– Bullying is the intentional picking on someone to hurt or upset them. Bullying can be physical, verbal, emotional, racist or sexual.

People can say strange things about bullying. Often these things are untrue but are said in denial or to comfort the speaker.

> "I was bullied and it didn't do me any harm"
> *"You'll just have to learn to stick up for yourself"*
> *"It's character building"*
> *"It's only name calling – that doesn't really hurt"*
> "That's not bullying – they're just teasing"

This is nonsense. Bullying is NEVER a good thing. It always damages.

Did I bring the bullying on myself?

You may be feeling small and useless. You may be feeling angry and victimised. One of the first things you may be thinking about is WHY? 'Why was I bullied?' and 'Why did they do it ?' Often you might feel like blaming yourself . . . DON'T!

Bullying is the bully's fault; no-one else's.

Repeat this to yourself as often as you like. Stick it on a poster, write it on your toothbrush, your clothes-hangers, your purse or wallet . . . It's true and it's important that you believe it.

Bullying happens because the bully has a problem and they take it out on others.

> ***'Crying is good medicine. It's like you know how the sky goes black and the air hangs heavy before a summer storm ? And then, after the thunder and the rain, there's a lovely, clean feel to everything.Well, crying can be like that. It clears the brain.'***

2

Famous People

An amazing collection of talented & famous people have been bullied. They have managed to put their bullying experiences to one side and move on successfully. Some say that they have used the bullying experience to power themselves.

Steven Spielberg . . . overcame bullying by casting his bully in a home movie. Spielberg admitted, "I used to fear going to school. I used to fear getting pounded by the bigger kids. I used to fear being humiliated on the baseball field. I used to fear having my heart broken by gorgeous babes who wouldn't date me. I used to fear everything".

Kate Winslet . . . was nicknamed "blubber". She explains that "I was very chubby as a child and I got much fatter in my teens. I was bullied for it, and found it hard to cope. The thought of going to the same secondary school as my tormentors terrified me, but my family helped me through."

Gillian Anderson, actress, was bullied when she moved with her parents to London.

' I am somebody and the universe is mine.
I am somebody and the universe belongs to me . . . too!'

Anthea Turner, presenter, disclosed that "there were times when I came home in tears. It was really eating me up. They used to call me names like 'posh' and 'stupid'. It did upset me".

Robson Green, actor said 'When you go through something like that, you know inherently that it's wrong. It seems to me that violence only breeds violence and that's true whether it's in the schoolyard or on TV.'

And there are many more examples . . .

Tom Cruise (actor), Harrison Ford (actor), Ranulph Fiennes (polar explorer), Mel Gibson (actor), Amanda Ross (TV presenter), Frank Bruno(boxer), Duncan Goodhew(Olympic swimmer), Michelle Pfeiffer(actor), Daryl Hannah(actor), Phil Collins (singer), Sir John Harvey Jones(industrialist and T.V. presenter), Lenny Henry (comedian), Patsy Palmer (actor).

You are not alone with your experience . . .

Kidscape carried out the first nationwide survey of bullying several years ago. Four thousand children aged 5 – 16 were interviewed from a random selection of fourteen schools.

The children were asked what worried them at school. Most of them (68%) said that they had been bullied at some times at school. 38% said they had been bullied more than once or had experienced a particularly nasty bullying incident. 26% admitted that they had at some time, been so severely bullied that they were terrified of going to school. They often played truant, pretended to be ill to avoid school or were made ill by the bullying. Some attempted suicide.

'Don't let the present be flooded by the past.'

How bullying can make you feel

Recently, Kidscape completed the world's first retrospective survey of the long-term effects of bullying.

The results of this survey show that bullying in childhood can go on to affect an adult in many ways, including:

- low self-esteem
- difficulty in making friends and maintaining relationships
- under achievement in education and the workplace
- anger, resentment and bitterness towards the bullies
- suicidal thoughts and/or attempted suicide

In fact, most of the quotes you will find in this book come from the people who took part in this survey.

"It may sound petty and like minor incidents to others. But words can get in your head and mess around with who you think you are. The words can stay there haunting you. The challenge is to emerge from it all into a healthy person."

It is important to get your feelings about the bullying out in the open but also to put them into perspective.

Try not to hold the bullying responsible for everything you don't like about yourself.

Use this book to think through the issues, deal with the leftover feelings and move on to be the person you are and want to be.

You might feel similar to some of the people who wrote to us

"I left school when I was 14 because I could not face the torture that I knew was waiting for me behind the school gates. I used to be physically ill at the thought of going to school, but my Dad would force me out the door. I would get my books and pretend to go to school, but the minute I turned the corner, I went off to a secret place where I could hide. My Dad told me to stand up to them – easier said than done when they were older, stronger and more cunning than me".

"I tried to kill myself when I was 14 by swallowing every tablet in the bathroom cabinet. My Dad found out and took me in to hospital. I spent a long time in a psychiatric hospital and suffered irreparable liver damage. I begged my parents not to make me go back to the school, which had an excellent reputation for academics. Thank goodness, they agreed. My Dad then took me to another school which was much better"

'My bullying at school was bad but my parents seemed to support it. They put me down so I felt as if everyone was. I got the bullying at school and even more at home. I have learnt that life isn't just about parents and school. You can and will meet wonderful, truly beautiful people out there and it is possible to shake off all the negative feelings you once had. Now, if someone offers me a negative feeling, I reject it and move on.'

"I learnt not to get angry. I taught myself not to cry. It took several years. Even now I can't cry . . . I still feel very intense pain. The intensity of the feeling is quite difficult to describe – it altered my perspectives. For years I have felt dirty, degraded and ashamed and at times, I feel intensely lonely. I get bouts of depression and anxiety attacks. Sometimes, for no apparent reason, I'll start shaking. These attacks are terrifying. I shake and sometimes hyperventilate."

'My life has shown me that no one can ever be sure if they are going to be a success. Anything can happen. Anything can go wrong or right. Success can often be a matter of chance. To wipe out hope by verbal, spiritual or physical aggression strikes me as one of the worse crimes of all."

'Bullies are cowards. They often operate in groups and get a feeling of power by upsetting others. Don't believe anything they tell you. Whatever they say, they are saying it to make themselves feel good. They are the sad ones - they can only feel good by being awful.'

You might find a way out through poetry or reading.

You might like to try writing a poem. It doesn't need to rhyme or to be any particular length. Write a few words you'd like to use, then join up some words to make up some phrases and work out a rhythm.

Use free form. Don't feel restricted to any conventions.

'My escape has always been inside my head. I use poems and daydreams, images and humour; these are my escape routes and they're always available.

Dealing with Anger

One of the issues that survivors of bullying have to deal with and often struggle with, is anger. Of course you're angry - you may have been through humiliation, name-calling, been ostracised, had limbs broken or otherwise been injured. You may have been subtly threatened in a way that you could not define, but which made you feel powerless, desperate and lonely. All of these experiences can leave you with a reservoir of anger that can be destructive, to those around you but most of all to yourself. So, let's look at anger:

Anger is a much-misunderstood emotion. It can be thought of as "not nice" or an emotion that always leads to violence. Neither of these statements is true.

What we do with anger can be positive or negative. Use it to motivate yourself to do something positive. One famous television presenter used her anger to power her way to success. When she met the girl who had been vile and violent to her, the girl no longer recognised her. The presenter introduced herself. 'How?..' said the ex-bully, who was snarling and spitting at the mouth, 'did someone like *you* ever get into a position like this ?' 'Oh that's easy to explain,' said the presenter. 'It was because of people like *you* that I found myself and found my way' and she walked on, head held high!

Unfocused anger which could have been expressed to those who injured you (if you'd had the opportunity) can stay with you and can turn inward resulting in depression, self-blame and even self – harm.

There is a story of a young man at the job centre who was spoken to rudely by a member of staff. The man, Theo, thought about saying something but then said nothing and simply left the centre. The angered burned. The man went home and was unusually quiet. 'Why are you so quiet ? ' said his mum 'You never share your feelings with me' and the anger burned in him and her feelings hurt in her. Later, the young man's younger sister, Debbie came home. 'How was the job centre?' said Debbie and Theo said nothing and the anger burned and the sister hurt. Moments later, the cat strolled into the room and jumped into the man's lap. The man felt so terrible that he hit the cat, sending it flying across the room. He had never before hurt the animal and could not understand why he had. Can you ?

Like Theo, we may store up our anger, letting many irritating incidents build up into a reservoir of unexpressed rage which eventually erupts like a volcano on those around us. Have you ever taken out your anger on people who do not deserve your outbursts and risked losing a valued friend or relation, while the real targets of your anger remained blissfully unaware of your feelings ? The trick is to get rid of the anger safely, offload it onto the person responsible or convert it into something *constructive* so it works to make *our* lives better.

*'We don't see things how they are,
We see things as we are.'*

Letting off steam

Sometimes, when something is driving us absolutely mad, we feel a need to let off steam. You might feel a need to hit someone or something, drive your car too fast or do something that's self-harming. At this point, be aware of the tension you feel and signal at yourself to stop. Now do something harmless with your aggression;

- Use a punching bag or beat a pillow or a cushion.

- Scream. (Into a pillow or cushion to muffle the sound – one survivor of bullying had three policemen rush to the house as a neighbour had called them thinking that there was a murder going on. In fact the person was simply expressing his anger.) You could try shouting in a car in a safe, quiet spot (with the windows closed – when STATIONARY!)

- Go for a run or a brisk walk.

- Write down everything you feel in words or images; however you feel you can best release it. If you write a letter, you don't need to post it, just write it to get the destructive feelings out of you.

Once you have got rid of the anger, you may still be feeling little, weak or worthless. So next, we have to challenge this.

'At the time, there may have been nothing you could do to stop the bullying, but now you can do everything. You owe it to yourself to fight back emotionally. Be better than the bullies. Be more successful. Be certain that they won't ruin your life.'

Use this space to start to let go of your bruises.
You may wish to write about them
Draw them
Or
Turn them into colours
You may just wish to stop and think.

'Our bruises will fade if we allow them to. We have choices. We can accept all criticisms and our negative self- image or we can start to be discriminating and to let the negative image GO . . . .!'

Boost your morale . . .

Write down all the positive things people have said about you.

Keep the comments that
you like on a poster or in
easy-to-see places, like on
your mirror on in your wallet.

*'I only recently realised that people I meet now won't see me the
way the kids in school did. You can be anyone you want to be.
They won't know the taunts. I won't let the present be eclipsed by
the past.'*

Remembering the child you were

Some people who have been bullied or hurt find it helpful to think back to what they were like before the hurt began. Over the years, as we have grown into adulthood, we have built up layers of behaviours and attitudes to protect ourselves from hurt and pain and to hide our true selves from possible ridicule or abuse. Bullying particularly can force us to hide our true thoughts, feelings and interests from others. We may have grown so used to pretending that things don't hurt us and that we don't care what people think about us that we have lost touch with what we really feel, what we really think and where our interests truly lie. Beneath our layers of coping mechanisms and pretence is the child we once were before the bullying began.

If you look at a small child, you can very often see the natural joy, self-confidence and self-worth that seems to exude from them. Some people we spoke to said that they found it useful to think back to when they had felt that natural joy and to nurture those feelings back into their current lives.

The task ahead of us is never as great as the power behind us.

These are some of the activities and TV programmes that were remembered as particularly enjoyable.

Age 3

Cuddling my dog
Jumping in puddles
Button Moon
Bagpuss
Play School
Muffin the Mule
(I fed the penguins)

Ice cream
Magic Roundabout
Emu
Mr Benn
The Clangers
The day at the zoo
Going to the seaside

Age 7

Cutting up shapes
Making collages
Birthday Parties
Chips

Making mud pies
Conkers
Night rider
Scooby Do!

Age 12

Computers,
Snogging,
Playstation

Dungeons and Dragons,
Fishing,
Grange Hill

What sort of things did you enjoy doing before you were bullied ? Perhaps you could give yourself one hour of play time per day or per week in a private place where you could safely indulge in those activities. It could be anything from playing the kazoo to making mud-pies – whatever !

I love and approve of myself

It's important to remind yourself that you're OK. You are enough.

Now, without inhibitions, make a list of all your good points that you know. You may want to choose words from our list. Or you may want to make up your own:

Active
Fun
Friendly
Spiritual
Trustworthy
Kind
Sensitive
Honest
Funny
Compassionate
Calm
Peaceful
Accepting
Daring
Loving
Loyal
Interesting
Creative
Thoughtful
Wild
Wise
Intelligent

Now, turn your list in to a portrait of you "ideal self". In your portrait, describe all your most positive qualities . . . .no negative ones allowed!

'I find that repeating to myself 'I AM GOOD ENOUGH'
just before going to sleep, is really helpful.'

What are your dreams . . . . . . ?

Paint this page with all your dreaming . . . .

'Accept. Float. Let time pass.'

What blocks your dreams . . . ..?

What stops you from seeing the sunshine and feeling the happiness ?

What gets in the way ?

You can, when you are ready, when it feels right, cut your blocks out and throw your blocks away.

'Happiness is like a butterfly, which when pursued, seems always just beyond your grasp, but which, if you sit down quietly, may alight on you.'

Now, list everything that you need to achieve your dreams . . . .

Put everything you feel you need into the shopping basket

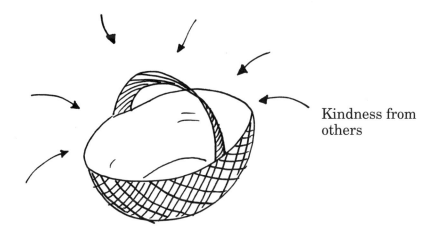

Kindness from others

This list is good to reflect on.

Some needs you may feel able to ask for from people close to you such as 'Please can I have some more hugs. They pick me up when I feel low' or 'Let's have a cup of tea' if you're shy about hugs.

Others you may need to develop yourself. Such as 'A belief in myself'

Others still, you may feel you need but then you might realise you already have it. Such as ' Strength to confront people when they've put me down'

'If a child lives with criticism, he learns to condemn; if a child lives with hostility, he learns to fight; if a child lives with ridicule, he learns to be shy; if a child lives with tolerance, he learns to be patient; if a child lives with praise, he learns to appreciate; if a child lives with encouragement, he learns confidence; if a child lives with security, he learns to have faith; if a child lives with approval, he learns to like himself; if a child lives with friendship, he learns to love the world.'

'Extract from Children learn what they live' by Dorothy Law Nolte

Write down everything that already makes you feel, even the tiniest bit
lovable and capable.

Mine would be..
Certain friends,
Certain family,
Certain music, ...
Hot chocolate
Bear hugs
Walking in bluebells,
Climbing a steep hill

'As soon as people saw I could stand up for myself, they respected
me more and treated me better.'

. . . What's yours?

Once you start to believe you are lovable and capable, you may wish to learn how to assert yourself to others. Even if you don't yet believe that you are lovable and capable, you may wish to learn how to be assertive so other people treat you respectfully.

Assertiveness is the ability to present yourself in a valued and positive way.

Assertiveness is about standing up for yourself in a non-aggressive way. Assertiveness is about stating your needs without infringing on the rights of others.

Assertiveness doesn't change your personality but gives out clear messages about what you will and won't accept.

- To be assertive start by deciding what is important to you. Make a list of what you think your rights are. Your list might include the following:

- The right to be taken seriously and the right to be listened to.

- The right to refuse requests – to say NO without feeling guilty or that you are being selfish.

- The right to make requests – the other person also has a right to say No.

- The right to make mistakes & the right to make our own decisions.

- The right to be myself without embarrassment or regret.

- The right to be free from physical aggression and intimidation.

- The right to ask for more information if we don't understand.

Keep your list of rights in mind when you are dealing with people. If you can't remember them all, choose one or two to focus upon. You can also help to develop your assertiveness by :

- Planning and practicing what you would like to say and/or how you wish to come across

- Keeping your requests clear and simple. You'll find remembering requests easier. Keeping situations simple helps others understand where you're coming from.

- Counting to ten or twenty when you feel stressed or overexcited. It really does help!

- If you're feeling angry, clenching your fists and then slowly releasing them. Concentrate on how your body feels as you do this. For each clenched fist, gather up all you anger. As you release the fist, you also release all your anger and tension. This is a great way to keep feeling calm and in control.

- Using the 'Broken record' technique is exactly what it sounds like! When a person asks for something that you are not prepared to give or do, you simply say so. For example; "I can't do -------------" or "I'm not going to ---------". You repeat what you have said as many times as you need to, no matter what the how persistent the other person is. Hence the title of the exercise.

- Trying 'fogging'. Fogging is when you are in a situation when you are feeling victimised. You imagine that a protective fog surrounds you. This acts as a shield. It starts at you feet and wraps itself around you body. You feel snug and safe. Your protective fog safeguards you from the comments that are being made. The fog helps stop the comments from penetrating. At the end of each day, you can unzip yourself from the fogsuit and put a new clean one on the next day ! Try this technique next time you feel vulnerable.

- When people try to make you feel bad, plucking up the courage to say something. They may not realise the effect of their words or actions on you. Be clear about what you need to say. You might say:

"When you do/say ----------- I feel --------------. Could you please bear this in mind/not do this again/ be aware of my feelings/----------.

This phrase is short and to the point. It makes it clear that you have feelings and the persons' words or actions are undermining to you. If they argue back or disagree, stand your ground. You could repeat what you have said or comment on the fact that you are not being listened to. Then walk away. You have made your point and stood your ground. The rest is their problem!

' BE EXACTLY WHO YOU WANT TO BE. '

COURSES

- Look for local organisations that run assertiveness courses. The following places may have details:

See the useful organisations listed at the back for specific groups information.

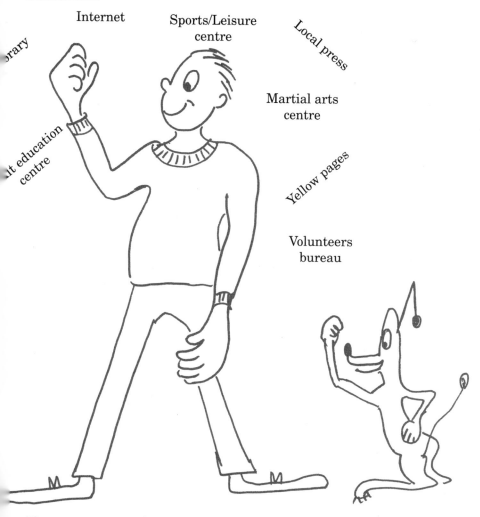

Internet

Sports/Leisure centre

Local press

Martial arts centre

Yellow pages

Volunteers bureau

rary

lt education centre

No-one gets every situation right all the time. Assertiveness is a skill that can take some time to develop. And there will always be some people who you don't get through to. Don't 'beat yourself up' about it.

' FEEL THE FEAR AND DO IT ANY WAY.'

Body Language

How do you hold your body and present yourself to others ? Do you seem interested, confident, relaxed, uptight, worried, happy, safe ?

Think about the different ways that people present themselves:

What they say,	'Please can I have a . . . Oh Sorry, Would you mind, didn't mean to bother you, but could you get off my foot ?' . . . .'Please get off my foot, it hurts'. 'Oh, hello' ' How good to meet you.'
Whether they make eye contact,	Distant gaze / Staring at floor Direct but friendly look
How they hold themselves,	Stooped and making themselves look tiny, Bold and upright, chest out, head up.
Look	Relaxed / Nervous / Stern / Friendly

You might ask friends for their comments on how you first appeared to them or for their help. Check out how you see yourself in the mirror. Perhaps, try copying confident, relaxed people's body posture. See what their position feels like.

You might try the relaxation exercise in conjunction with this exercise.

'Bodies hold feelings. Let them go'

Relaxation

If you have learnt to survive with cruelty and anxiety around you, you may have learnt to hold some of it in your body. Just as you reflect on how the bullying has affected you emotionally, you may wish to look at how it has made you feel physically.

It is important that you can feel safe within your community and within your body. You might try the following:
Stand in a comfortable room where you will not be disturbed.
Have some pillows or cushions to hand.
(Switch the phone to answermachine, put the cat out and have only relaxing music)
(Put an alarm on if you might fall asleep.)

Stand with your feet shoulder-width apart.
Now turn your attention to your body.
How does it feel ?
Which parts feel tight ? which relaxed ?
Do you feel balanced ?
Are you taking up the space in the world that is yours ?

(You might trying closing your eyes to focus on the feelings)

Slowly work your way down your body by thinking about an area and relaxing it.
You could try scrunching up your shoulders or stomach muscles then letting them go, to get a sensation of relief in that area.

Breath deeply and comfortable.
Breathe slowly alllowing the air to come in . . . and out.
In and out.
You may feel this is enough for one session or may want to repeat this a few times.

Then, if and when you feel ready, try lying on the ground face up, of course! Let the floor take your weight. Let the floor carry you. If it is uncomfortable lying flat, put a pillow under your knees and head.

When you feel relaxed, let yourself actually feel the sensation. Close your eyes. Tell yourself how good it is to feel and be safe and comfortable, warm and relaxed. Try to remember this feeling so next time you feel yourself tensing up, you can get your body back to the relaxed, calm state. Take up the space you need. As you get used to using this relaxation, you may wish to repeat positive ideas to yourself once you are most relaxed. You might try 'I am safe. I am OK. I am lovely,' or whatever you wish.

'I realised I judged people by how they seemed, so I determined to appear as I wished to be perceived.'

Owning your feelings

Sometimes we don't ask for what we want and then we get upset when we don't get what we want. Much argument and misunderstanding can be avoided by simply owning our feelings and perceptions and communicating them to the other person.

Sometimes we can get angry with someone because we assume that they are doing something for a certain reason; perhaps because they don't like us or don't care about us. Rather than instantly assuming they have a bad motive and accusing them of not liking us or going away with our secret fear unexpressed, we can check out the reality of the situation.

The best way to do that is by making "I" statements.

"I *feel* . . . . I *think* . . . . . .

This gives us the chance to say how we are feeling and what we think the other person is doing and for the other person to say what is actually going on for them.

Here's an example:

When my boyfriend comes in from work he hardly smiles, barely says "hello" and disappears into the other room without showing any interest in me. After this has happened several times, I tend to get angry with him and say "Every time you come in from work, you scowl at me and ignore me, you don't like me anymore." Sometimes I'll swear too!

This response is likely to get an angry response back and ,hay presto, two people upset!

Instead, I could express my feelings by saying "when you come in from work and you don't smile and you don't ask me how I am, I feel angry and upset because I think you don't like me anymore."

This way, the other person has more of a chance to give their view of the situation and we find out that actually they have been having a very hard time at work recently and they come in tired and just want to be on their own for a while. We might also learn that their mood has nothing to do with·us!

'If you always say what you mean, you'll always mean what you say.'

There are certain situations where saying "I feel Angry" may not the best thing to do. For instance, it could cause havoc with your boss or a police officer or a stranger who doesn't know you. This is because so many people have the negative belief mentioned above that anger means violence and think they're about to get hit!

Try channeling your anger into another activity:

- Sport – beat hell out of that squash or tennis ball rather than someone else (It'll save you getting a criminal record or a broken nose!)

- Political or voluntary activity, all that energy could go into making changes in the world that you would like to see.

- Any activity that makes your life better, putting yourself at the top of the list, making yourself number one for a change.

You owe it to yourself to use your anger constructively,
Because you're worth it!

'If you find it hard to do nice things for yourself, pretend that you are someone else and decide how you might look after that 'other' person. You might try giving yourself flowers, making yourself a cake, making yourself a card or taking yourself to a favourite spot.' Go on, try it!

Counselling or Therapy

One way you can start to deal with your feelings is through seeing a counsellor; someone with whom you might confidentially discuss your feelings and concerns.

Counsellors can be found in several ways:

- referral by your GP (free)
- the telephone directory. Yellow pages has a section on counselling
- contacting organisations like the British Association of Counselling or Youth Access (see A – Z of Help)
- local volunteers bureaux may have local counselling organisations

What type of counselling is available?

Getting out there . . .

Many survivors of bullying find it difficult to get or keep a job. This could be for a number of reasons: low self – esteem, feeling unemployable, fear of being bullied again, having had an interrupted education due to bullying and lack of qualifications.
We may feel that our experiences or skills or talents (and yes, everyone has them) are worthless and couldn't possibly be useful to anyone. Alternatively, we could have a wealth of qualifications behind us but we still feel useless and that we have nothing to offer to an employer.

To counter this feeling, it can be useful to write several lists down in brainstorming sessions:

'I found enormous release in going to see a counsellor and talking confidentially regularly.'

1) On the first list, write down everything that you have done that has ever earned you money or could possibly earn you money. This can range from the very simplest thing that you learned to do when you were a child through to the most complex. Include on the list things that you might not want to do for a living but could bring in some money if you really were desperate.

The list could look like this:

Baking a cake

Lawn-mowing

Driving

Singing

Listening to someone

Taking the dog for a walk

Babysitting

Cleaning

Tutoring

Decorating

Sewing

Digging a hole

Negotiating

Answering the telephone

Word-processing

This may seem pointless, but it's amazing how this simple exercise can transform your view of yourself and your money - making ability. There are many people who either don't want to or don't have the time to do some of the above things for themselves and who are willing to pay someone else to do those things for them. Someone, for example, like you.

'Starting work in a new place was really cathartic. No one knew me, no one knew about the bullying, I learnt new skills and got structure into my days.'

Now try yours -

2) Now write another list – write down all those things that other people say you are good at or you know that you are good at. If you can't think of anything, perhaps ask someone you know to help you. The list may include some of your previous list or something you've not thought of yet.

'Talk to people you trust. Take it as slowly as you feel comfortable. Learn who you find dependable.'

3) Write down a list of all your positive personal qualities. Consult the list you made earlier in the book. Everybody has them. Nothing negative about yourself is allowed on this list! Again, ask someone close to you to name some of your good qualities if you are having difficulty with this. If someone tells you that you don't have any, consider ditching them as a "friend!"

'Try to recall all the things people have complimented you on as clearly as you remember the bad stuff!'

4) And another one ! Write down places or ways of being that make you most comfortable in a working environment. Mine would be;

Loose clothing / no uniforms,

Friendly/unstressful

Small groups of colleagues in my team

Low level of noise (no blarring radios or tannoys)

What are yours ?

5) Another list! – write down all the things that you *love* doing. Earlier on in this book there was a section which asked you to think about what your dreams are – this could include what you dream about doing for a living.

Ensure whatever the weather or however you feel, you do something you enjoy every day.

When you have written these lists, reflect about what you have learned. I hope you will be more aware of your qualities and what you have to offer an employer.

Most importantly, pay particular attention to the last list - what you would really love to do in your work – . . . GO FOR IT!

Give yourself a few days or weeks to let the ideas sink in and swim around comfortably in your brain. It may take some time to get there, you may encounter obstacles and you may have to earn money some other way for the time being but wouldn't it be great to aim for what you really want to do?

Another useful exercise is to spend some time looking at job advertisements in the newspapers. Cut out any that interest you. Don't focus on the ones you are qualified for. Cut out *any* which catch your eye and make you think 'I wonder . . . !' You should find you have a collection of various jobs and careers.

Now think of what skills you already have which you could offer that employer. Are you able to apply for the job? Do you need to get particular qualifications or skills? Whatever the answer is to these questions you have achieved something. You have short listed jobs and/or careers that you would like to pursue, this gives you goals.

In order for you to establish what extra training or experience you need you may need to take some of the action suggested in the following section.

Getting qualifications

In "Useful Organisations" you will find a list of people you can contact about education opportunities. In addition there are lots of local places you can go to find out about further education:

- Library
- Adult Education College
- Job Centre
- Local press
- Careers centre
- Internet

As an alternative you might want to get in touch with the Workers' Education Association. They are the largest voluntary provider of adult education in the United Kingdom. There are over 650 branches, which provide in excess of 10,000 courses each year.

The WEA provides access to a wide range of educational opportunities, from accredited courses to courses studied for the satisfaction of learning something new and meeting others.

Anyone can join a WEA course. *You do not need previous qualifications or experience, only curiosity and interest.* Courses offered by branches include: history, literature, music, creative arts, ecology, philosophy and many others.

Things to bear in mind . . .

- If you're not sure how to get a job talk to people you know who are employed and are *happy with what they do*. Ask them how they found their job. Ask them about the interview. Ask them what they would recommend you should do to obtain work. Perhaps most important, ask what pitfalls to look out for.

- If you know exactly what you'd love to do, ask around. You might even put the request on your answermachine 'Hello, thanks for calling. I am out looking for work as a waiter/apprentice plumber. If you know anyone looking for one, please leave me the details along with your message.. Thank you. BEEP!'

- When you approach an interview don't think, "What do I have to say or do to get this job"? This question implies that you have already made up your mind that this *has* to be the job for you and that they only have to like you. Remember that the interview is a chance for you to check out the organisation and the people in it. *You are on trial. But so are they.*

- Talk yourself 'up'. Employers will genuinely want to hear about your strengths. They want to know what you can offer. Remember – be honest and balanced. You may want to talk about some 'weaknesses' but remember to promote yourself in a positive light. You might want to ask how the company how they will support you as you skills develop. That shows you are interested in staying long-term too. If you are worried about the interview, practice with a friend or family member or write down possible questions on scraps of paper, turn them over randomly and answer them clearly out loud.

- Don't pin all your hopes on one job. If you don't get it you'll feel very low about yourself. Always have alternatives. Alternative jobs to go for, alternative things to say in an interview, alternative ways of describing what you want . . . . If you have a particular job or organisation that you want to work in, write to them and tell them that you would like to work for them, this is called a "speculative approach". It is one of the most successful methods of getting a job as the employer knows that you are genuinely interested and not just applying for any old job. It is useful to get a name of somebody in the organisation so you can target them.

The way most people get their jobs is by word of mouth. Tell everybody that you come across that you are looking for a job.

Good luck!

'YOU CAN DO IT! IT MIGHT TAKE A WHILE . . . BUT YOU CAN AND WILL!'

Writing a letter

Many employers have reported that one of the reasons that people fail to get a job with them is that their initial approach by letter has let them down because it was not well written. Letters of complaint are also more effective if well written. Letter writing is an important skill and you will gain a lot by writing a letter that is well set out and clearly and simply written.

On the next two pages are standardised letters that can be used as a model for any job application or letter of complaint.

'Learning to write was a big breakthrough for me. I was determined that the bullies wouldn't stop me communicating with people forever. I am even doing an evening course in writing now. I keep a file of letters and framed my first voluntary job offer.'

DRAFT JOB APPLICATION

YOUR NAME AND ADDRESS
YOUR PHONE NUMBER (INCLUDING DIALLING CODE)

THEIR NAME

THEIR ADDRESS

. . . .

. . . .

THEIR POSTCODE

DATE

Dear Mr / Mrs . . . .

Re: Position of cashier, Daybury's
as advertised in the Daily Echo, 24 June 2000.

I am very interested in the position of cashier for Daybury's and would
be grateful if you could consider me for the job. I am particularly keen
to work there because I think you have a great range of fresh produce
and friendly staff.

I have experience cashing up as I worked in a bar throughout 1997 and
more recently helped fundraise for a volunteer organisation, the
Hedgehog Handout.

I have enclosed a brief CV for your information.
I so look forward to hearing from you,

Sincerely,

Helen Coombs

If you are writing to a named person, write 'Yours sincerely,'
If you are writing a Dear Sir or Madam letter, write 'Yours faithfully,'

DRAFT CV

ARIEL BAKER

Flat 2, 5 Aylmer Close, Sixoaks, London SW29 5PG
Telephone No. 0171 730 7081

Date of birth: 24 June 1979

Overview
Ariel is a very able man with particular interpersonal skills.
He has a keen interest in service relationships and customer care.
Ariel is a good all-rounder and works well in teams.

Education

Brownes School, Edgbaston	1995 4 G.C.S.Es English, Mathematics, Art, Biology
Significant roles:	Member of Middle School Choir, French Exchange Programme 1994. Football team member.
Career:	1996 Cashier – Harry's Newsagents Responsible for delivery of papers to 68 homes. Sole responsibility for daily stock check Ongoing service relationship with customers Liaison with suppliers 1997 – 1998 Warehouse Shift Worker– Diggles Warehouse Responsible for weekly stock check Packing heavy goods for delivery in Europe.
Voluntary Roles:	Coaching for local estate Under 11s Football team Hospital radio record selector, Wednesday evenings
Hobbies and Interests	Music listening, Cycling and keeping fit.

DRAFT LETTER OF COMPLAINT

THEIR NAME   YOUR NAME
THEIR ADDRESS   YOUR ADDRESS
. . . .
. . . .
THEIR POSTCODE   YOUR POSTCODE

DATE

Dear Mrs Apple,

MOULDY CHOCOLATE BARS

On 12 April 1999, I bought 5 chocolate bars from 'The Sweet Shop' 2 Hammock Road, Reality, Barnes. They cost me £1.50 in total.

When I opened the first bar I found, to my horror, that the bars had gone mouldy.

I have looked at the other bars and found them to be identically affected.

I would be grateful if you would consider recompensating me for the bars. I enclose one bar for your inspection.

Thank you very much for your help in this matter.

Yours sincerely,

Hans Barhard

'Affirming my rights, even about seemingly insignificant matters has helped me feel that I matter to other people and I matter to myself.'

- If it is a formal letter and the recipient is likely to receive many such letters, on different topics, help him by giving the letter a heading, e.g. Cashier Post./ Item for sale or whatever the letter is about. If the letter should use a reference number, put it in the top right, where it is clearly visible. This helps the person reading the letter if they have to answer many letters of a similar type for different positions.

- Always use a formal sign-off 'Yours faithfully' or 'Yours sincerely'

- Keep all letters as brief, clear and simple as possible. Try to fit all you want to say on one side of A4 paper. An employer will want to employ someone who can communicate clearly and stick to the point.

- If replying to a job advertisement. Remember to say which job you are applying for, often an organisation is trying to fill two different posts at the same time. , Start by saying when and where you saw the advert. eg. Lifeguard Position, as advertised in The Guardian, 17 May 1999.

- In your CV, remember to put in the roles or responsibilities that you have had which will be particularly useful in the job for which you are applying.

- Make your job application letter polite, formal but friendly. Employers want to work with people they think will do the job well and be a good colleague.

- Write out a letter in rough first, crossings – out don' t look good. It is a good idea to take a photocopy of an application form and fill that in, in rough before you fill in the one that you will send. If you feel your handwriting is small or scruffy, try filling in forms in neat, block capitals. Use as smooth a pen as you can. Check for spelling mistakes and any other errors in your letters before you write them out and send them off. Get someone else to look over them as well if possible.

- A letter of complaint needs to be as short as possible. A long letter can give an impression of being a professional whinger! State clearly the nature of your complaint and ask for what response you would like, e.g. a refund, an apology or an opportunity to talk to the person you are writing to. Ask for a reply within a certain amount of time.

- Keep a photocopy of the letter and CV you send. You may be asked questions about what you have written in the interview.

At the end of this book, there is a list of books on job-hunting and letter-writing.

REMEMBER YOU ARE NOT YOUR JOB

If you would like to do more with your time or are finding it hard to plan your day or to get up in the morning . . . you might try

Taking up a sport.

Joining a new club.

Taking up an alternative interest: line dancing, yoga, eel fishing, mountain climbing, pot – holing.

Working as a volunteer. Your local Volunteers Bureau will tell you how you can help.

Take a close look at your friends. Do they treat you the way you would like to be treated or has your self esteem risen and you have found that some of the people around you don't reflect the new you? If you are looking to improve your social life check out the befriending or dating agencies. They might be a good way to expand your social scene.

Or get a part time job in a place where you know you'll meet like – minded people. Restaurants, bars or pubs. The money may not be fantastic but you'll probably have a laugh.

Inspiration

Throughout this book, we have written quotes from individuals about what they have found helpful. Below are books, songs, films and quotes that people found particularly inspiring and healing.

Songs:
"Something inside so strong" – LABI SIFFRE. "I believe I can fly" – R KELLY
"We have all the time in the world" – L ARMSTRONG. "If I can dream" – ELVIS
"State of Independence" – DONNA SUMMER.   "I am what I am" – G GAYNOR
"Don't worry, be Happy" – BOBBY MCFERIN
"Higher Ground" – JOHN DENVER. "I will survive" – GLORIA GAYNOR
"When I am back on my feet again" – MICHAEL BOLTON.
"Return to Innocence" –ENIGMA.
"The Greatest Love of All" – WHITNEY HOUSTON
 "Bridge over troubled water" – SIMON AND GARFUNKEL
"I've gotta be me" – SAMMY DAVIS JUNIOR
"The best things in life are free" – LUTHER VANDROSS/JANET JACKSON
"Bad obsession" – GUNS 'N' ROSES
"Everybody hurts" – R.E.M.
"Don't give up" – PETER GABRIEL AND KATE BUSH
Adagio for strings – SAMUEL BARBER
"Deliver me" – D REAM
"Stand by me" – BEN E. KING
"Hero" – MARIAH CAREY
"Search for the Hero" – M PEOPLE
"You gotta" – DESIREE
"You are not alone" – MICHAEL JACKSON
"You'll never walk alone" – GERRY AND THE PACEMAKERS
"The only way is up" – YAZZ
"Things can only get better" – D:REAM

Films:
"Oliver" – originally a book by Charles Dickens.
Chariots of Fire
Kes
Gregory's Girl

Poems:
"If" – Rudyard Kipling.
"A farewell" – Charles Kingsley.

Quotes:
"We do not see things as they are. We see things as we are" (The Talmud)
"The Lord is my Shepherd, I shall not want" (Psalm 139)
"Though I walk through the valley of the shadow of death the Lord is with me" (Psalm 23)
"I lift my eyes up to the hills, but where shall I find help? My help comes from the Lord who made Heaven and Earth" (Psalm 121)
"Therefore if any man be in Christ then he be a new creation, the old has gone, the new has come" (2 Corinthians 5:17)
"Grant us the serenity to accept the things we cannot change, the courage to change the things we can and the wisdom to know the difference."
(Reinhold Neibuhr. Serenity Prayer)

A – Z of helpful organisations . . .

Alcohol
Alcoholics Anonymous
Stonebow House
Stonebow
York
YO1 2NJ
Tel: 01904 644026

Al Anon/Alateen. For anyone, friend or relative
affected by someone else's drinking.
61 Dover Street
London
SE1 4YF
Tel: 0171 403 0888

Alcohol Counselling service
34 Electric Lane
London
SW9 8JJ
Tel: 0171 737 3579/3570

Drinkline
13 – 14 West Smithfield
London
EC1A 9DH
Helpline: 0171 332 0202

Bereavement
The Compassionate Friends
(for parents whose children who have died through accident, illness,
murder or suicide)
53 North Street
Bristol
BS3 1EN
Helpline: 01272 539639

Cruse
(offers counselling for all bereavement)
126 Sheen Road
Richmond
Surrey
TW9 1UR
Helpline: 0181 332 7227

General Counselling
British Association of Counselling
1 Regents Place
Rugby
Warwickshire
CV21 2VT
Tel: 01788 578328

Rape Crisis Centre
(see telephone directory for local numbers)
Tel: 0171 837 1600

Drugs
ADFAM (families and friends of drug users)
Waterbridge House
32 – 36 Loman Street
London
SE1 OEE
Tel: 0171 928 8900

Cocaine Anonymous
(Information, literature and details of group meetings)
Helpline: 0171 284 1123

The National Drugs Helpline
Tel: 0800 77 66 00
        (24 hours)

Narcotics Anonymous
(Literature, listings, information)
Helpline: 0171 251 4007
(10am – 10pm)

Eating Disorders
Overeaters Anonymous
(can also help bulimia and anorexia nervosa)
Helpline: 01426 984674

Eating Disorders Association (EDA)
Sackville Place
44 – 48 Magdalen Street
Norwich
NR3 1JU
Tel: 01603 621414

The National Centre for Eating Disorders
11 Esher Place Avenue
Esher
Surrey
KT10 8PU
Tel: 01304 841700

Smoking
QUIT
Tel: 0800 002200

Solvents
Re – Solv
30a High Street
Stone
Staffs
ST15 8AW
Tel: 01785 817885

Samaritans
Telephone: 0345 909090

Youth Access
1a Taylors Yard
67 Alderbrook Road
London
SW12 8AD
Tel: 0181 772 99

Education and Training

WEA
Call: 0181 983 4840
Ask for the Education Officer for information on your local WEA branch

The Basic Skills Agency
Call: 0800 700 987

National Council for Voluntary Organisations
Call: 0171 713 6161

National Association for the Care and Resettlement of Offenders
Call: 0171 582 6500

For information on courses. These are available to anyone, not only offenders nation-wide!

Special Needs . . .

SKILL
National Bureau for students with disabilities
336 Brixton Road
London
SW9 7AA
Tel: 0171 274 0565

Disability Law Service
Room 241, 2nd Floor
49 – 51 Bedford Row
London
WC1R 4LR
Tel: 0171 831 8031

Self defence
The Ki Federation of Great Britain
(will give local numbers)
Tel: 01278 641166

Adult Bullying
Bullies can be found anywhere and we all come across them. Here are some useful contacts if you are being bullied in adulthood.

Andrea Adams Trust
Shalimar House
24 Derek Avenue
Hove
East Sussex
BN3 4PF
01273 417850

National Workplace Bullying Advice Line
Success Unlimited
PO Box 67
Didcot
OXON.
OX11 0YH

01235 834548
http:www.successunlimited.co.uk/PTSD/.

Recommended Reading:

I'm OK, Your OK! by John Berne

Healing the shame that binds you by John Bradshaw

'The Artists Way' by Julia Cameron

'You can Heal Your Life' by Louise Hay

'Women who love too much' by Robin Norwood

'Letters from Women who love too much' by Robin Norwood

'A Creative Companion' by Sark

'Feel the fear and do it anyway' by Susan Jeffers
'101 Ways to Deal with Bullying' by Michele Elliott

(see how your school or parents could have dealt with it!)

Job-seeking:
'What Colour is your Parachute?' by Richard Nelson Bolles.

All about Kidscape

Kidscape is a registered charity committed to keeping children safe from bullying and abuse.

Kidscape offers :

* Training for groups of teachers, parents, carers, police, LEAs in behaviour management, anti-bullying policies and child protection. All training is tailor made to suit the group's specific knowledge and needs.

* A helpline for parents of children being bullied at school Monday – Friday 10am – 4pm.

* A series of 3 free booklets on bullying is available from us by sending an A4 80p SAE to:
Kidscape , 2 Grosvenor Gardens, London SW1W ODH

* Advice and research into ;
Longterm effects of bullying (£3)
The link between Young Offenders and Bullying (£2)
What Sex Offenders Tell Us (£3)
These are available in return for a cheque and SAE.
Please ensure you write which one you want..

* We also have a range of books and posters.
Send an S.A.E to us marked ORDER FORM to Kidscape

If you would like to contact us, please write to

Kidscape
2 Grosvenor Gardens, London, SW1W ODH

Call us on 0171 730 3300 Fax us on 0171 730 7081
www.kidscape.org.uk

The last word should go to the many people who wrote in who have gone far beyond bullying . . .

' I realised that it was their problem and that, if I looked closely enough and listened hard enough, I was fine: I am fine. From then on, everything was so much easier. '

' I found someone who didn't notice the nasty things and only saw the positive. It took ages before I could trust what she said but I found enormous happiness through her and how she perceived me. Now I am working on how I see myself and I am learning to trust that.'

'I felt that I was 'over it' the day my daughter first went to school. I didn't really worry about her all day. Even better was the moment she left the school grounds and said what a great time she'd had. I can't tell you how wonderful that was.'

'Please, tell people that they are enough, that they have the character and talent to be and to succeed. Tell them that certain days will be hard but they'll pass and tell them to go to sleep at night repeating positive messages to themselves. One day, I promise, they will realise the bully had the problem and that they are free of the bully, free of the problem and they can move on confidently and happily. There is a life of positivity beyond bullying.'

ACKNOWLEDGEMENTS

This book is the result of thousands of people's input.

We would particularly like to thank Nicola Bale, Thaddeus Birchard, Angeline Brook, Megan Bruns, Katharine Chapman, Paul Day, Samuel Day, Neville Eisenberg, Ian de Ath, Souad Faress, Megan Fenwick, Lisa Flowers, Alice Garrett, Roderick S.Graham, Anne Halpin, Daphne Joiner, Emmanuella Lartey, Eileen Lee, Ivan McFie, Andrew Morrison, Geraldine Mushett, Valerie Phillips, Steve Ranford-Bragg, Claire Roberts, David Schuster, Jackie Skipper, Alan Speers, Mark Taha, Barbara Taylor, Ian Youngs.

The beautiful illustrations are by Roz Eirew who volunteered her wonderful characters and fabulous enthusiasm for this book.

We would like to acknowledge all the bullied people who helped us with our survey and called our helpline, all those who have participated in Zap and all those who didn't.

NOTES